MW01146458

Hey Kids! Let's Visit Savannah Georgia

Teresa Mills

Life Experiences Publishing

Bluff City, Tennessee

Teresa Mills/Life Experiences Publishing
PO Box 53
Bluff City, TN 37618
www.kid-friendly-family-vacations.com

Book Layout © 2014 BookDesignTemplates.com

Hey Kids! Let's Visit Savannah Georgia/Teresa Mills -- 1st ed.
ISBN - 978-1-946049-02-5

Contents

Preface

Welcome

Savannah, Georgia, is one of the most beautiful Southern cities in the United States! Savannah is a smaller city, and you can really see quite a bit by just walking around. Like so many other places that you can visit, there are just so many things to do and see there.

This book is written as a fun fact guide about some of Savannah's attractions. Throughout the book I include some history interspersed with fun facts about things to do in and around the city. Parents can either read the book with their children or have their children read it themselves.

You can visit Savannah, Georgia, right from your own home with this book! You can enjoy this book whether you are preparing for a vacation with the family and want to learn more about the city or just wanting to learn a little more about Savannah.

When you take your family trip to Savannah, I have a free gift to help you plan! Go to this link to receive your gift:

http://kid-friendly-family-vacations.com/savannahfun

When you have completed this book, I invite you to enjoy the other books in the series. We visit Washington DC, a Cruise Ship, New York City, London England, San Francisco, Paris France, Charleston South Carolina, Chicago, Boston, Rome Italy, Philadelphia, San Diego, Seattle, Seoul South Korea, Atlanta, and Dublin Ireland!

Enjoy!

Teresa Mills

Introduction

A Little About Savannah Georgia

Welcome to Savannah, Georgia!

Savannah, Georgia, is a Southern city full of history and natural beauty. The downtown historic district was originally laid out in a grid fashion to make it easier for the militia to practice drills. This plan made way for the building of twenty-four beautiful city squares. Twenty-two of those city squares remain today. Savannah's city squares are thought of as the city's jewels.

You will revisit history and go back to the time of the American Revolution and the American Civil War as you visit museums, forts, and even cemeteries.

There are many things to do and see in Savannah. In the downtown area, you will find many places to wander and explore. There are city tours to take that will fill you in on the deep history of this "oldest city" in Georgia.

So, are you ready?

Let's visit Savannah, Georgia!

1

Savannah City Squares

The Savannah Historic District contains twenty-two park-like squares (originally there were twenty-four, but only twenty-two remain). The squares vary in size and layout. Each square really has its own personality. Savannah's City Squares are thought of as the city's jewels.

Below are descriptions of the city squares located in downtown Savannah.

Calhoun Square

In 1851, Calhoun Square was laid out and named in honor of John C. Calhoun, often called the Great Orator of the South. Surrounding the square are many beautiful homes that were built with a Greek revival theme.

Chatham Square

Located in a neighborhood on Barnard Street, Chatham Square was designed in 1847 and was named after William Pitt, better known as the Earl of Chatham or the Great Commoner. Just like Calhoun Square, Chatham Square is surrounded by beautifully built Greek revival-styled houses.

Chatham Square

Chippewa Square

Considered the most popular of the twenty-four city squares of Savannah, Chippewa Square is the heart of the city's business district. Restaurants, theaters, and other popular business spots surround this square.

Chippewa Square was designed in 1815 in recognition of the Battle of Chippewa during the war of 1812. A statue of James Oglethorpe stands in the center of the square.

Chippewa Square is also famous because in the movie *Forrest Gump,* Forrest Gump sat on a bench in this square waiting for a bus.

Chippewa Square

Columbia Square

This square was designed in 1799 and named for the popular nickname of the American Colonies. It is located right in the middle of the city's downtown streets but is a quiet place among the daily hustle and bustle, characterized by a fountain located right in the center.

Columbia Square

Crawford Square

Named in honor of William Harris Crawford and designed in 1841, Crawford Square boasts a basketball court and a gazebo. That is a lot to fit into a small city square. It is now the only Savannah city square that still has a fence around it.

Elbert Square

This square, named after the Revolutionary soldier turned Georgia governor Samuel Elbert, is now a small sliver of grass between Hull and Perry Streets. Elbert Square was designed in 1801 in honor of Samuel Elbert (a Revolutionary soldier who later served as governor and sheriff). It is one of the twenty-four squares that was lost during the city's development. It was sold to help fund a citywide cistern project.

Ellis Square

Originally, this square was given the name Market Square because of the four public markets that were in the square. In 1954, Ellis Square was destroyed to be turned into a parking lot, but fortunately, in 2005, the parking garage was torn down and the square was rebuilt.

There is a fountain located in Ellis Square that is a favorite spot on a hot day for locals and tourists.

Franklin Square

Franklin Square, located right in the middle of downtown, is the center of nightlife in the city. It was designed in 1790 to honor Benjamin Franklin.

Greene Square

This square is located on Houston and President Streets. Greene Square was built in 1799 in honor of Nathanael Greene. He was an American Revolutionary War hero. Greene Square has a relaxing atmosphere, making it the perfect spot for both locals and tourists to gather.

Johnson Square

This is the oldest and the largest square. Located at the junction of Bull and Saint Julian Streets, Johnson Square was named after the royal governor of South Carolina, Robert Johnson. It is the center for social gatherings and often considered the most beautiful building in the city's downtown.

Lafayette Square

Lafayette Square

Named in honor of Marquis de Lafayette, Lafayette Square is where the Cathedral of Saint John the Baptist and Semiquincentenary Fountain, a fountain presented to the city for its 250th founding anniversary, are located.

Liberty Square

Laid out in the 1700s, this square was paved to construct the Chatham County Courthouse and the Robbie Robinson Parking Garage. This is another of the original twenty-four that no longer exist today.

Madison Square

This square is named after US President James Madison. In this square, vintage cannons from the old Savannah Armory are found. Because of how vintage the place is, this square is home to some of the different haunted tales that surround around the city.

Madison Square

Monterey Square

Monterey Square was laid out in the 1800s to honor the 1846 Battle of Monterey that took place during the Mexican American War. In this square stands the monument of General Casimir Pulaski.

Oglethorpe Square

Once known as Upper New Square, Oglethorpe Square, designed in 1742, features benches lining the city's brick sidewalk.

Oglethorpe Square

Orleans Square

Established in 1815 and named after the Battle of New Orleans, this square is home to the German Memorial Fountain, which commemorates the role of the early German immigrants during the rise of the colony of Georgia.

Pulaski Square

Pulaski Square was named after the eighteenth-century freedom fighter and Polish general Casimir Pulaski. This square was one of the later added squares as a part of the grid expansion.

Pulaski Square

Reynolds Square

Named in honor of John Reynolds, Reynolds Square is the perfect place for people to gather after spending time at the musical theaters, restaurants, and ice cream parlors located around it.

Telfair Square

Home to Trinity Methodist Church, Telfair Square, along with the Telfair Museum of Art and the Jepson Center for the Arts, were named after Edward Telfair and his family because of their contribution to the city's growth.

Troup Square

Although small in space, this does not stop the beauty of Troup Square from shining through. This square contains the Armillary Sphere, a sphere that was originally invented by the Greeks and used by ancient astronomers to track celestial orbits and see the pattern of equinoxes and solstices.

Warren Square

Named after a Revolutionary War hero named General Joseph Warren, this square is home to the Spencer-Woodbridge House.

Warren Square

Washington Square

Once a garden, Washington Square, named in dedication to the first president of the United States George Washington, is now the perfect spot to sit and just enjoy the scenery surrounding the square.

Washington Square

Whitefield Square

Though hard to believe it was once a burial ground, Whitefield Square is now home to a Victorian gazebo and beautiful azalea flowers.

Wright Square

Wright Square

In this square stand two monuments: the monument of William Washington Gordon and the monument of Tomochichi. William Washington Gordon was the first mayor of Savannah. Tomochichi was chief of the Yamacraw Indians. He worked closely with James Oglethorpe when he settled in the area that later became Savannah.

Fun Facts about the Savannah City Squares

- Each square has at least one landmark (historical building or church), monument, memorial, or fountain and i named for a person or historical event.

- The Savannah city squares are part of the city's history. General James Oglethorpe laid out the city in a grid fashion.

- There were originally twenty-four city squares, but due to the city development, only twenty-two remain.

2

Savannah Historic District

Located south of the river, the Historic District of Savannah is home to old mansions, homes, live oak trees, fountains, monuments, and the city squares, all of which played a crucial role in the development of the city's history and the growth of the city itself, along with the people living in it.

History

The Savannah Historic District was built based on the concept of wards. A ward consisted of a square and the surrounding 8 blocks. Each ward had a central square and was given four trust lots and four tythings. The trust lots were to be used for civic purposes—a church, a museum, a school, etc. The four tythings, or tithings, were each subdivided into ten residential lots.

Horse in City Market

Filled with the beauty of the city's history, the Historic District of Savannah is alive with eighteenth- and nineteenth-century architecture and green spaces. Even the restaurants, cafés, homes, theaters, boutiques, galleries, museums, churches, and mansions that can be seen today are rich with the historical vibe.

Fun Facts about the Savannah Historic District

- Monuments, houses, restaurants, ice cream parlors, and many other buildings that surround the Historic District of Savannah have a mid-nineteenth-century revival style.

- The Historic District is known for the haunted tales that surround it.

- The wars that took place in the city in the past contributed a lot to the richness of the city's history, as well as to the city's culture and economic growth.

3

River Street

Once century-old buildings and old cotton ware-houses, the structures on River Street have been converted into colorful boutiques, galleries, res-taurants, cafés, inns, hotels, and a lot more.

The Riverfront Plaza

The Riverfront Plaza was once abandoned but was fortunately rediscovered by people who wanted to revive River Street, taking it back to the time of its golden age. This then led to the renewal of the area and its growth.

River Street Buildings

The Olympic Torch

The Olympic Torch Sculpture located on the river-front symbolizes the American spirit of victory and athletic competition. It is designed with five columns that serve to represent the five Olympic rings and billowing sails that represent and commemorate the Olympic yachting events that took place in the city during the 1996 Summer Olympic Games.

Morrel Park and the Waving Girl Statue

The bronze statue of the waving girl standing in Morrell Park portrays the image of Ms. Florence

Martus and her collie dog, both residents of Savannah. Ms. Martus is the embodiment of hospitality because of how she was always seen greeting every ship that entered the ports of Savannah. The statue serves as a tribute to her and a symbol of eternal hospitality.

Riverfront – Waving Girl Statue

Water Taxis

Water taxis are ferry boats that allow both locals and tourists to visit Hutchinson Island located at the opposite side of the river.

Fun Facts about River Street

- The Savannah River Street is paved with two-hundred-year-old cobblestones.

- The Savannah River forms most of the border between South Carolina and Georgia.

- The buildings along River Street were once cotton warehouses.

4

Forsyth Park

Savannah's Historic District has one of the most popular parks in the US, Forsyth Park. It is home to the Confederate Monument (a memorial to Savannah's Civil War dead), completed in 1879. The bronze statue on the top of it is the work of David Richards, a sculptor from New York.

It was William Brown Hodgson who had the idea of creating a recreational park in Savannah. He donated ten acres of wooded land for this purpose. In 1851, the thirty-third governor of Georgia, John Forsyth, donated twenty acres more, bringing the total size to the park's current size. The addition was made in 1867.

Forsyth Park – Confederate Monument

William Bischoff designed the original landscape of Forsyth Park. Improvements to the park were made in the 1850s. Iron fencing was added. Ornamental plants and walkways were built to replace old pine trees. After that, the great fountain in the park was also added.

Originally used as a military parade ground, dummy ports were built on it in 1909, and the park itself was used as a training site for soldiers during the First World War.

Forsyth Park Fountain

Fun Facts about Forsyth Park

- The fountain in this park is not only famous for its beauty. It is a place for romance. Countless marriage proposals, engagements, couples photo shoots, and even weddings use its fountain as a background. The fountain is 159 years old.

- Forsyth Park covers 30 acres and is the largest park in the Savannah Historic District.

- The park is named for John Forsyth (33rd Governor of Georgia) who donated 20 acres to complete the park in 1851.

5

Juliette Gordon Low's Birthplace

The Juliette Gordon Low Birthplace is a museum in the Savannah Historic District. It recently received an honorable mention citation from the American Alliance of Museums for its library exhibit and celebrated its sixtieth founding anniversary as the Girl Scout headquarters in the US. The Birthplace was dedicated for Girl Scout causes on October 19, 1956. In 1965, it was honored as the first historic landmark in Savannah.

This building was constructed originally as the home of James Moore Wayne, the Savannah mayor at the time. The mayor later became a US congressman and a Supreme Court Justice.

Wayne later sold this to Juliette's grandfather, William Gordon I. Juliette was born in this house on

Halloween in 1860. Gordon is the man behind the founding of the Central of Georgia Railway. The purchase of the house for the Girl Scouts was made in 1953.

Girl Scout trips, visiting schools, and families are welcome to tour the Birthplace.

Fun Facts about Juliette's Birthplace

- Juliette still has a living relative who comes to the Birthplace every now and then. Being a relative of the Gordons, she can touch anything in the house.

- Juliette's nickname was Daisy, and she started the first troop of Girl Scouts in 1912.

- The garden outside the house is a project of the Girl Scouts.

6

Historic Churches: First African Baptist

The First African Baptist Church is considered North America's first African American Baptist congregation. The church also operates a museum displaying eighteenth-century memorabilia. Located on Franklin Square, the church is west of the City Market.

Reverend William J. Campbell supervised the church's completion. The church building was constructed beginning in the 1800s (finished in 1859) by both slaves and free African Americans. After slaves worked the day in the fields, the builders made bricks and erected the church. The church was the first brick building to be owned by the state's African American residents.

First African Baptist Church

The upper balcony has some original pews crafted by slaves. On the furniture's sides are tribal symbols of those who made them. In the early twentieth century, the church's original bell tower was destroyed by a hurricane. As a contributing property for the city's historic district, the church building is listed in the National Register of Historic Places.

The church holds weekday tours. The church is one of Savannah's most visited places, especially when it comes to historical artifacts. One of the church's attractions is the pipe organ, which dates to 1832.

The First African Baptist Church is still used as a place for worship. As a community leader, the congregation helps people who require aid. Its programs have undoubtedly changed the lives of local residents.

Fun Facts about First African Baptist Church

- The church sanctuary's historical stained-glass windows were installed during the pastorage of the church's fifth pastor, Reverend George Gibbons. The windows can still be found along the building. A stained-glass window installed during the time of

Reverend George Leile (1773) can still be found in front of the church.

- The church's ceiling is in the Nine Patch Quilt design, representing that the church was a safe place for slaves to seek sanctuary.

- The church was the largest gathering place for whites and blacks to meet during segregation. In the city, some blacks were not permitted to march with their fellow graduates. Rather, they had separate ceremonies held at this church.

- Below the floor of the lower auditorium is a finished subfloor—the Underground Railroad. The entrance still is unknown. After leaving the tunnel, slaves—as much as possible—would attempt to head north.

- The sanctuary has inspired notable people like civil rights activist and actor Lou Gossett Jr., Grammy Award–winning singer John Mellencamp, former US Vice President Al Gore, Reverend Jesse Jackson, Wally Amos, and Debbie Allen.

7

Historic Churches: Cathedral of Saint John the Baptist

The Cathedral of Saint John the Baptist, a Roman Catholic cathedral, is located at 222 East Harris Street and is the Roman Catholic Diocese of Savannah's Mother Church. As one of Savannah's most awe-inspiring structures, the style is French Gothic.

The Cathedral was first built in 1873 and was dedicated on April 30, 1876. The spires were 1896 additions. The Cathedral was nearly destroyed by a fire on February 6, 1898. The Cathedral's interiors were destroyed, while the two spires and the outside walls were spared.

Cathedral of Saint John the Baptist

In 1904, stained glass windows by Innsbruck Glassmakers were installed. Murals were later painted. The murals and the stained-glass windows are several reasons why the Cathedral is one of the city's landmarks.

The Cathedral was again restored from 1998 to 2000. During this time, the murals were restored, a new baptismal font and altar were made with Carrara marble, and a new pulpit featuring the New Testament's four evangelists were added.

Fun Facts about the Cathedral of Saint John the Baptist

- Also known as the Sistine of the South, the Cathedral is filled with marble-like columns and stained glass. The church's thirty-four murals are some of its best features. The murals, dating back to 1912, are oil-on-canvas paintings transferred to the walls of the church.

- The murals are filled with symbolism. While each mural has an important Christian feature or saint, the details are worth a look. Many figures hold items like keys, body parts, and palm leaves. Most Cathedral tour guides know about each mural's trivia and facts.

- An interesting feature is the headless Saint Denis of France, who is carrying his own head. Legend has it that people did not like the saint's preaching. The people decapitated him. The interesting part in the legend is that the saint picked his head up and continued walking and preaching.

- Other interesting murals detail Saint Lucy holding an eyeballs-filled plate and a Native American theme. Before her execution, Saint Lucy's eyeballs were ordered removed. The Native Indian mural is dedicated to Saint Isaac Jogues, the first martyr of North America. He was attending to the Native Americans in southern Canada and New York and was captured by the Mohawks and killed. What is interesting is that a person wearing Native American garments in Catholic Church art is unusual.

8

Historic Churches: Congregation Mickve Israel

You may think that the Congregation Mickve Israel is a Christian church. Its Gothic architecture includes pinnacles, slightly pointed windows, and stained-glass windows. The current church, built in 1876, is found on Monterey Square and deemed an icon of the Jewish community in Savannah.

If you want to learn more about the history of Jews in Georgia, the Congregation Mickve Israel is the place to go. Although the original congregation members established the synagogue in 1735, it wasn't until 1818 that the congregation erected its first building. The wooden structure was burned down in 1829. A brick synagogue was built on the same site and consecrated in 1841.

Eventually the brick structure was no longer able to accommodate the congregation's growing numbers. So, construction of the current synagogue was begun in 1876; the synagogue was completed and consecrated two years later in 1878.

Starting in 1868, the congregation transitioned from traditional worship to Reform Judaism. To fully shift to Reform Judaism, in 1904 the congregation joined the Union of American Hebrew Congregations.

Members of the congregation continue to enrich the nation and community with their presence in fields of law, commerce, government, military, culture, and politics.

Congregation Mickve Israel offers tours for visitors to see the synagogue and the museum. It is one aspect of Savannah's spiritual and cultural life that should not be missed.

Congregation Mickve Israel

Fun Facts about the Congregation Mickve Israel

- Early and recent objects and documents pertaining to Jewish life in the city and the rest of Georgia are displayed in the synagogue's museum. Of interest are the fifteenth-century Torah as well as letters to the congregation from US Presidents Jefferson, Washington, and Madison.

- The synagogue is the United States' only purely Gothic revival synagogue. It was consecrated in 1878 and designed by Henry G. Harrison. The building is listed on the National Register of Historic Places.

- The congregation is the country's third oldest Jewish congregation and the South's oldest Jewish congregation. Its founders comprised the largest Jewish group to settle in the continent in the colonial period. In July 1733, the founders arrived in the city onboard the *William and Sarah*. Members of London's Bevis Marks Synagogue financed the journey.

- Of the forty-two congregation founders who arrived from Europe, thirty-four were Sephardic Jews of Portuguese and Spanish origin. They had survived the Portuguese and Spanish inquisitions and lived as Marranos (Jews who secretly practiced Judaism but pretended to be Catholic). The rest were Ashkenazic Jews of German descent.

9

Historic Cemeteries: Bonaventure Cemetery

Located at 330 Bonaventure Road in Savannah, Georgia, Bonaventure Cemetery is one of Savannah's most visited landmarks.

The cemetery is in a place that was originally a plantation south of the city. John Mullryne owned the original plantation. William H. Wiltberger established the Evergreen Cemetery Company on June 12, 1868. The city bought the cemetery and the land on July 7, 1907 and renamed the area Bonaventure Cemetery.

Bonaventure Cemetery Cross

The cemetery is the burial place for several well-known personalities. One well-known person buried in the cemetery is singer-songwriter Johnny Mercer, who is buried in the cemetery section near the Bull River. Conrad Aiken is also buried in Bonaventure Cemetery. He grew up in Savannah, where he wrote some of his poems and novels.

Gracie Watson, who died when she was only six years old, is also buried in Bonaventure Cemetery. Her father commissioned a sculptor to create a lifelike statue in her honor. Her burial site is one of the cemetery's most visited graves. The grave is fenced in with wrought iron, and the grave is nearly always adorned with stuffed animals, flowers, and trinkets to make a child happy.

Admission to the cemetery is free. However, there are paid tour guides who will dig into the history of the cemetery with you. The paid tour covers the graves of famous Georgians and other interesting people.

Transportation is normally included, and tourists will also see the cemetery's older section and walk along the bluff that overlooks the Wilmington River.

Bonaventure Cemetery

Fun Facts about Bonaventure Cemetery

- John Muir, an American naturalist, slept for six nights at the cemetery in October 1867. He felt that the cemetery was the cheapest and safest accommodation that he could find in the city.

- The cemetery was featured in author John Berendt's best-selling book entitled *Midnight in the Garden of Good and Evil*. The book's cover featured the Bird Girl sculpture, which is now located at the Telfair Museum of Art.

- The cemetery is also a Holocaust memorial. In 1950, 344 victims of the Holocaust were brought over from a Nazi camp. They are buried in the cemetery's Lot 415.

- During the Siege of Savannah in 1779, before the site became a cemetery, the place was used as a military camp, military hospital, and landing site. Thus, unknown military personnel were buried in the cemetery.

10

Historic Cemeteries: Colonial Park Cemetery

In the heart of Savannah's National Landmark Historic District is the Colonial Park Cemetery, at the corner of Abercorn Street and Oglethorpe Avenue. The cemetery, with an area of almost six acres, is the burial place for some of the city's earlier residents. The cemetery was previously known as the Old Brick Graveyard, the Old Cemetery, Christ Church Cemetery, or South Broad Street Cemetery. From 1750 to 1853, it was the city's main public cemetery.

Colonial Park Cemetery

As Savannah's oldest preserved municipal cemetery, Colonial Park Cemetery is a popular site for visitors. The cemetery contains over nine thousand graves, including that of Georgian signatory of the US Declaration of Independence Button Gwinnett. William Scarborough, the old owner of the Savannah Steamship Company, is also buried in the cemetery, as is the country's foremost miniatures painter, Edward Green Malbone.

In 1896, the Park and Tree Commission started the beautification process. The Trustees Garden Club, in 1967, undertook a vital restoration project. In 1990, the city initiated a preservation project to maintain the cemetery for the succeeding generations. The public can enter the cemetery daily from 8:00 a.m. to 8:00 p.m.

Fun Facts about Colonial Park Cemetery

- Over seven hundred victims of the Yellow Fever Epidemic of 1820 are buried in the cemetery. Also buried are numerous victims of the city's dueling era, wherein the first dueling death was in 1740 and the last death was in 1877. Some of the duels were fought around and in the cemetery.

- No Confederate soldiers are buried in the cemetery as it was closed to burials before the Civil War's beginning. During their Savannah occupation, Federal troops took over the grounds and many of the graves were desecrated and looted. There's also talk that the Union soldiers altered many headstone dates.

- The cemetery is a popular ghost tour attraction. Even one walking tour dares entering the grounds at night. In a story, a maid at a Bay Street hotel was found in tears outside the cemetery's gate. When asked why, the maid said that she followed a man from the hotel who walked into the grounds and vanished.

- The cemetery is also home to one of the city's famous ghosts. A disfigured orphan, Rene Asche Rondolier, called the cemetery his home during the 1800s. Accused of killing two girls, Rene was dragged to the cemetery's adjoining swamps, lynched, and left for dead. In the following days, more dead bodies were found. The people of the town said that Rene's ghost was responsible, and they called the cemetery "Rene's playground."

11

University of Georgia Aquarium

Georgia's first saltwater aquarium, the University of Georgia (UGA) Aquarium is a state-of-the-art aquarium located on Skidaway Island, about 25 minutes from downtown Savannah. You can see a great deal of Georgia's marine life there.

The aquarium also features skeletons and fossils of animals that were taken from the bottom of the nearby river, the Skidaway River. The fossils are those of woolly mammoths, whales, sharks, mastodons and giant armadillos.

A Truly Educational Trip

Along with the fun of watching marine life in the aquarium, the UGA has an auditorium and hosts educational activities for kids. There are two teaching laboratories—a computer lab and an art lab.

Sea Turtle (in its natural habitat)

Other Fun Things to Do

- Nature Trails: Ask the staff about Jay Wolf, the enthusiastic volunteer after whom the nature trail of the site was named.

- Saltmarsh Boardwalk: This is the opportunity to observe wildlife from observation platforms.

- Skidaway Learning Garden: This is a great site for learning about the plants native to

Georgia coasts. The site has magnificent plants taken from the Georgia coastline.

- Birding: This is one of the best birding sites for tourists. There are feeder sites and picnic bluff sites for this purpose. Wading birds, waterfowls, and songbirds dancing in the air and singing their enchanting music are a great sight to behold.

Fun Facts about the University of Georgia Aquarium

- The University of Georgia Aquarium is Georgia's first saltwater aquarium.

- The aquarium houses over 50 species of Georgia's marine life and also has a touch tank with snails, turtles, fish and crab.

- The UG Aquarium has a boardwalk around the Skidaway River - you can observe more of the marsh-life on this boardwalk.

- The aquarium has an underwater camera system that allows visitors to see the marine-life up-close.

12

SCAD Museum of Art

The SCAD Museum, located in the Savannah Historic District, provides a showcase for some of the finest works of contemporary art. It is also a teaching museum designed to enrich the education of students at the Savannah College of Art and Design. New exhibitions are unveiled every academic quarter, featuring works by celebrated professionals that not only draw art lovers from all over the world but also serve to inspire and challenge students to push their creative boundaries.

History

The museum was founded in 2002 in an 1856 Greek Revival building that was originally the Central of Georgia Railway headquarters. Originally named the Earle W. Newton Center for British-American Studies after a major collection of American and British art that was awarded to the museum as a gift, the museum was given its present name in 2006 due to the expanding nature of its collections.

In 2011, SCAD underwent the most substantial renovation in its history, with many new facilities being added. In addition to revitalizing its classrooms and galleries, the museum also now has a conservation studio, a 250-seat theater, an outdoor projection screen, a twelve-foot orientation digital touch screen in the form of a table, and a café. The entrance to the museum also features an eighty-six-foot glass-and-steel lantern that greatly enhances the city's skyline.

Collections

The museum is home to the Walter O. Evans Collection, one of the largest collections of African American art in the country. There are works by Richard Hunt, Romare Bearden, and Edward Mitchell Bannister, as well as the Earle W. Newton Center, which houses antique maps and rare books by artists such as Thomas Gainsborough and William Hogarth. Its permanent collection of over 4,500 pieces includes works by Pablo Picasso, Salvador Dalí and Annie Leibovitz, as well as haute couture by Oscar de la Renta, Yves Saint Laurent, and Chanel.

Fun Facts about the SCAD Museum of Art

- The eighty-six-foot lantern in front of the museum was intended by designer Christian Sottile to symbolize the rebirth of the structure that houses it after decades of neglect and decay.

- The museum used seventy thousand repurposed "Savannah Gray" bricks from the original structure, which were handmade by slaves before the Civil War.

- At the time it was built, the twelve-foot interactive digital table was the largest such device in the world intended for public use.

- The museum was designed to be environment-friendly, with low-energy light fixtures, low-flow plumbing to reduce water use, zoned climate control and exterior cooling towers, as well as low-emission glass used on the south elevation.

13

Leopold's Ice Cream

Leopold's is a Savannah institution that has been serving residents since 1919. In addition to its famed homemade super-premium ice cream, which is shipped all over the world, it also serves a delicious menu of sandwiches, soups, salads, and freshly baked treats, which are all made from scratch. Leopold's is located at 212 E Broughton St, in the historic section between Reynolds Square and Oglethorpe Square.

History

Peter, George, and Basil founded Leopold's after immigrating to America from their native Greece. An uncle who was already living in the US introduced them to the art of dessert and candy making, and they were soon developing their own secret formulas.

The Leopold brothers opened their first parlor on the corner of Habersham and Gwinnett, where two streetcar lines intersected. It became an instant hit, and locals still talk about the banana splits, malts, and milk shakes served by the soda parlor. Their ice cream and sherbet molds became a fixture in Savannah's finest clubs, and the parlor became a popular hangout for students after sporting events, dances, and concerts.

Unfortunately, this original location was forced to close after Stratton Leopold, who had been managing the store, left Savannah to pursue a career producing Hollywood movies. However, Stratton reopened Leopold's at a new location in East Broughton Street, which was decorated in the style of a 1935 diner, including many of the fixtures from the original location such as the telephone booth and black marble soda fountain.

Presently, Leopold's continues to make its ice cream using the original recipes and techniques handed down to Stratton by his father, Peter. Its range of ice cream flavors includes classics such as Tutti Frutti, Peanut Butter Chippy, and Honey Almond and Cream, as well as seasonal favorites that are only available during particular months.

Fun Facts about Leopold's Ice Cream

- To celebrate its anniversary, Leopold's holds an annual block party where they serve single scoops of ice cream at just ninety-seven cents per scoop. The party is also an occasion for the community to show its support for the ice cream parlor that has become a local fixture by holding its own events.

- Leopold's continues to make its ice cream in small batches to ensure freshness, with any toppings and add-ons, such as nuts, folded in just before the ice cream is served.

14

Savannah Children's Museum

Located in Tricentennial Park at 655 Louisville Road, the Savannah Children's Museum was opened in 2012. The outdoor museum houses at least a dozen interactive exhibits that are exclusively for kids.

Children can explore, touch, and run through educational displays and join in daily activities. Highlights include a sensory garden, walk-through maze, musical instruments from around the world that are playable, building with LEGOs and blocks, story time, dress-up, and learning through play in the Exploration Station.

The museum occupies the lower level of the courtyard and the old shop, giving two levels of play and fun to be explored and enjoyed by the whole family. The museum property is one acre and opens in two phases. The first phase is the outdoor play space.

The museum also offers slides, jungle gyms, and many other attractions. The Savannah Children's Museum also has a reading corner filled with books for children of all ages to read. Lecturers are also around, and they offer daily programs to keep the families and children learning and exploring together.

Within the museum complex, kids can see an early twentieth-century train turntable that's still functioning, as well as historic diesel and steam locomotives. The railroad museum also has thirteen of the old railroad station's original buildings.

Fun Facts about the Savannah Children's Museum

- The museum is Savannah's first official children's museum. The current Savannah Children's Museum is especially created for kids but incorporates history and science, instead of the other way around.

- Exploration Station's downstairs area is set within the remains of the Central of Georgia Carpentry Shop, which was destroyed in a fire in 1987. The remaining Savannah Gray brick arches and walls were typical of 1850s local architecture when the shop was built.

- Exploration Station's upstairs level has an archaeology exhibit that lets kids learn about dry-digging and underwater archaeology by working their way through dry and wet sand to find "artifacts" that represent coastal Georgia's history, such as Revolution-era cannonballs and a shipwreck.

15

Skidaway Island State Park

Located near the Historic District of Savannah, this park has one of its borders on Skidaway Narrows. That border is part of the network of Georgia's waterways.

Trail hiking is one of the best activities to do there. The most popular trail is the one that winds through the maritime forest. After hiking the trail and walking past the salt marsh, you will see boardwalk platforms and an observation tower.

Other Fun Things to Do

- Time spent here can be very educational and even "wild."

- Wildlife viewing: One fun activity is birdwatching. You will also see other wildlife.

Look at animals in their natural habitat—
egrets, raccoons, fiddler crabs, and deer.

- Inside this park's interpretive center, you will find a window, reference books, and binoculars for birdwatching.

- Camping: The state park is a great spot to find a camping site under the live oaks. Leashed dogs and cats are allowed.

- Aquarium: Skidaway Island is home to the University of Georgia Aquarium.

Fun Facts about Skidaway Island

- One of the largest paintings in the world was painted here by the students of Savannah College of Art and Design. It was painted in 1995. Guess who is featured in that painting? It's Elvis, the King of rock 'n' roll.

- Sea turtles, an endangered species, come back to Tybee Island every year to lay their eggs. You may be able to catch them if you go there from May until October.

- The official bird of the island is the painted bunting.

16

Georgia State Railroad Museum

Located at West Broad Street and Railroad Avenue the Georgia State Railroad Museum is formerly known as the Roundhouse Railroad Museum. The Central of Georgia Railway handled maintenance, passengers, freight, and manufacturing at the site, which was built beginning 1850. There are thirteen original structures that remain standing to this day.

In 1833, the Central of Georgia Railroad was chartered, and by 1843, the company was the world's longest continuous railroad under one management. During the 1920s, the railroad reached its peak and continued to operate during the Great Depression. With the emergence of diesel locomotives, however, the railroad declined and ceased operations in 1963.

Georgia State Railroad Museum

The City of Savannah owns the museum, and the Coastal Heritage Society has operated it since 1989. Five of the thirteen existing buildings contain permanent exhibits, including the roundhouse and the turntable. Museum visitors can see model railroads, steam-powered machinery, rail cars, diesel and steam locomotives, and a brick smoke-stack (126 feet) with outhouses around the base.

Across from the museum is the Savannah Visitors Center, which was the former passenger station of the Central of Georgia Railway. Inside the building are displays of the city's history. Underneath the train shed is a Baldwin steam locomotive engine that was built during 1890.

Fun Facts about the Georgia State Railroad Museum

- The museum is considered the world's most complete and largest Antebellum-era railroad repair facility that is still functioning. Visitors can walk across the complex grounds where rolling stock is displayed, learn more about each building's purpose, and participate in scheduled activities that may include railcar tours, a train ride, the handcar, and activities for children in the baggage car.

- The museum's centerpiece is the eighty-five-foot turntable that has been functioning for over a century. The locomotive, for several times a day, operates and carries museum visitors on a short yet memorable ride. You can hear the sharp whistle, jets of steam, and the clang and clack of iron on steel.

- For over a century, the Savannah shops complex was a major Central of Georgia Railway repair facility. The museum is listed as a National Historic Landmark District and has been designated as the Georgia State Railroad Museum by the State Legislature.

17

Old Fort Jackson

Old Fort Jackson is the state of Georgia's oldest standing fortification made of brick. It perches on the Savannah River's banks, so guns installed in the fort could fire on vessels coming into Savannah.

As a National Historic Landmark, the fort is one of Savannah's must-see spots. Year-round, the fort offers cannon firings during weekends. From March through October, interactive programs are scheduled daily.

The fort is only minutes away from the historic district of Savannah. You will be able to see the Talmadge Bridge and the city's riverfront skyline as you walk through the fort.

Old Fort Jackson Cannon

Old Fort Jackson is significant as it's a completed example of Second System fort architecture and retains most of Captain William McRee's original design. Casements under the gun platform were used as office spaces, cells, and storage. A brick wall is behind the battery, with four demi bastions to allow extra defense angles. A moat surrounds the walls and battery, filled by way of a tunnel that runs through the Savannah River.

Mid-eighteenth-century modifications to the fort did not radically alter the fort's original features. The renovations entailed the replacement of wooden structures (like the original palisade and gun platform) with brick structures.

Signs and films about Old Fort Jackson offer historical background, and the fort staff can answer other questions. Owned by the State of Georgia, the fort is operated by Coastal Heritage Society as a museum.

Fun Facts about Old Fort Jackson

- Named after an American Revolution hero, James Jackson, construction on the fort began in 1808 and was finished just as the 1812 war erupted between Great Britain and the United States.

- Originally built of brick-faced earth and topped with a wooden-gun platform, the battery was one of the country's strongest fortifications. In March 1812, Captain William McRee of the Corps of Engineers reported that the battery was ready for the cannon mounting.

- Old Fort Jackson, as originally designed, consisted of the battery (semi-circular) that faces the river. Mounted cannons could control a long channel stretch.
- When Great Britain declared war on June 18, 2012, McRee stated that eight guns

were mounted. However, there were no soldiers to mount them. Meanwhile, militia troops from Georgia responded. In July 1812, Eighth US Infantry men garrisoned the post.

18

Fort Pulaski

Fort Pulaski is a national monument located on Cockspur Island. A popular destination for both history and nature lovers, the fort dates to the Civil War, when it was considered one of the most remarkable harbor defense structures in the country.

Fort Pulaski is noted as being the site where the Union Army first successfully used rifled cannons against masonry fortifications. The cannon caused substantial damage to the outer walls as well as completely breaching a corner wall, prompting the commander of the Confederate garrison, Colonel Charles H. Olmstead, to surrender rather than risk massive loss of life.

Fort Pulaski

The fort was later used as a prisoner-of-war camp, housing captured Southern troops, as well as a bar against Confederate goods being shipped from Savannah. It was designated as a national monument in 1924, when it was restored to its original condition, and became a unit of the National Parks Service nine years later.

Fun Facts about Fort Pulaski

- Hand-formed Savannah Gray bricks, which were made by slaves at the Hermitage plantation, were used in the construction of the fort.

- The fort was named in 1833 after Count Kazimierz Pulaski, who served in the Revolutionary War under George Washington and was killed in 1779 during the Siege of Savannah.

- The early phases of construction were supervised by young Robert E. Lee, a young second lieutenant, who designed the dike system and selected the site for the fort.

19

Tybee Island

Tybee Island is one of the most popular destinations in Savannah, especially for those who enjoy the sun and the surf. Located some twenty minutes from Historic Savannah, the island boasts five miles of public beaches fronting the Atlantic Ocean.

Tybee was originally claimed by Spain in 1520. However, the Spanish government was eventually forced to renounce her claim after superior British and French settlements were built in the area. British settlers led by General James Oglethorpe established the colony of Georgia in 1733 and named the area Savannah due to the tall grass and marshlands that were prevalent there.

Tybee Island Lighthouse Station

Due to its strategic location near the mouth of the Savannah River, a lighthouse was first built in its northern tip in 1736. At ninety feet tall, the Tybee Light Station was the highest structure in the US at the time. The original lighthouse has been replaced several times, although all of its original support buildings remain intact. At present, the lighthouse is one of the island's most popular tourist attractions.

Activities and Attractions

- Memorial Park is the perfect place for the family to spend a warm summer afternoon. The 4.5-acre park boasts of a playground, picnic area, and several sports courts, including outdoor beach volleyball and tennis courts, as well as a lighted basketball court. There is also a covered pavilion that can seat up to 150 people.

- The Tybee Marine Science Center shows that learning can be fun. The Center is dedicated to educating the public about the important of preserving the area's coastal resources. In addition to the Center's interesting exhibits, the staff also holds regular hour-long beach walks, marsh treks, and ocean seining (fishing with a dragnet) sessions.

- Little Tybee Island provides a wonderful opportunity to be exposed to nature in its unspoiled state. It is an uninhabited barrier island, reachable only by boat that is home to a variety of wildlife, including many rare bird species. Guests can go fishing, nature hiking, birdwatching, and picnicking.

Fun Facts about Tybee Island

- The US Air Force dropped a nuclear bomb near Tybee Island in 1958 following the collision of two planes during a military exercise. The bomb did not go off and has never been found.

- In the 1500s, Tybee Island was a popular hideout for pirates, who used the island not only to evade pursuers but also to hide their ill-gotten treasure.

- Tybee Island beaches are a nesting ground for endangered sea turtles that come ashore to lay eggs from May to October.

20

Ghost Tours

Savannah is a rich part of US history. It is brimming not only with culture but also with never-ending tales of horror. A journey to the most haunted spots of the city at night is a favorite among visitors.

Here are a few of the many ghost tours a tourist can enjoy in Savannah:

Ghosts and Gravestones

Journeying the streets of the city onboard the Trolley of the Doomed, the tour includes sightseeing and storytelling of the various old mansions and spooky cemeteries all around the city that once served as battlegrounds during war times.

Shannon Scott Tours

This tour allows tourists to have a once-in-a-life-time experience of entering Savannah's closed cemetery gates at night and be informed of Savannah's many bloody historical events that took place on those grounds.

Sixth Sense Savannah

This tour is probably the creepiest, yet at the same time the most thrilling, out of all the ghost tours in Savannah. In this tour, the guides do not simply provide tourists with measly stories of ghosts that roam around the city, but instead they cover the real darkness that happens behind the colorful buildings and streets by sharing knowledge about shadow people, exorcism, voodoo, and much more.

Hearse Ghost Tours

In this tour, tourists are transported from place to place in a hearse. But rather than an actual hearse, it is a transformed open-air vehicle. Although the roads may be rough, this does not stop the fright and excitement the ride brings as guests are shown the haunted buildings of the city while learning about the city's gruesome history.

Ghost Talk Ghost Walk

This tour is perfect for tourists who want to see and learn about the haunted places of Savannah while enjoying a leisurely walk around the city. In this tour, tales from the book called *Savannah Spectres and Other Strange Tales* are related by the guides. This tour also allows tourists to interview some of the residents of Savannah who have "seen" the ghosts.

Fun Facts about Savannah's Ghost Tours

- It is not true, as some ghost tours claim, that the bull's-eye-patterned bricks near the Colonial Park Cemetery have a connection to the occult.

- The number of bodies buried in the Colonial Park Cemetery in Savannah exceeds the number of the tombstones.

- Ghost tour guides in Savannah sometimes exaggerate the horrendous history of Savannah to creep out the guests.

I hope you enjoyed visiting Savannah. I have a free gift that you can download and enjoy as you plan your trip to Savannah, Georgia!

Kid-friendly-family-vacations.com/savannahfun

Please consider adding a review to help other readers learn more about Savannah, Georgia whether traveling or learning from home. Thanks!

Kid-friendly-family-vacations.com/review-savannah

Also By Teresa Mills and Kid Friendly Family Vacations

Hey Kids! Let's Visit Washington DC

Hey Kids! Let's Visit A Cruise Ship

Hey Kids! Let's Visit New York City

Hey Kids! Let's Visit London England

Hey Kids! Let's Visit San Francisco

Hey Kids! Let's Visit Savannah Georgia

Hey Kids! Let's Visit Paris France

Hey Kids! Let's Visit Charleston South Carolina

Hey Kids! Let's Visit Chicago

Hey Kids! Let's Visit Rome Italy

Hey Kids! Let's Visit Boston

Hey Kids! Let's Visit Philadelphia

Hey Kids! Let's Visit San Diego

Hey Kids! Let's Visit Seattle

Hey Kids! Let's Visit Seoul South Korea

Hey Kids! Let's Visit Atlanta

Hey Kids! Let's Visit Dublin Ireland

MORE FROM KID FRIENDLY FAMILY VACATIONS

BOOKS

Books to help build your kids / grandkids life experiences through travel and learning

https://kid-friendly-family-vacations.com/books

COLORING AND ACTIVITY PAGKAGES

Coloring pages, activity books, printable travel journals, and more in our Etsy shop

https://kid-friendly-family-vacations.com/etsy

RESOURCES FOR TEACHERS

Resources for teachers on Teachers Pay Teachers

https://kid-friendly-family-vacations.com/tpt

It is our mission to help you build your children's and grand-children's life experiences through travel. Not just traveling with your kids... building their "Life Experiences"! Join our community here:

https://kid-friendly-family-vacations.com/join/

Acknowledgements

Proof-reading / Editing

Deb Hall – TheWriteInsight.com

Cover Photos

Layfayette Square – © pilens / 123rf.com

River Front - Buildings - © appalachianview / deposit photos

Cathedral of St. John the Baptist - © James Pintar / 123rf.com

Tybee Island Lighthouse Station - © duckeesue / deposit photos

Photos in Book

Chatham Square - © pilens / 123rf.com

Chippewa Square - statue - © Darryl Brooks / 123rf.com

Columbia Square – © Hackman / deposit photos

Layfayette Square – © pilens / 123rf.com

Madison Square - © fotoluminate / 123rf.com

Oglethorpe Square – © fotoluminate / deposit photos

Pulaski Square - statue - © Darryl Brooks / 123rf.com

Warren Square - © fotoluminate / 123rf.com

Washington Square - © fotoluminate / 123rf.com

Wright Square - © dbvirago / deposit photos

Horse in the City Market - © dbvirago / deposit photos

River Front - Buildings - © appalachianview / deposit photos

River Front – Waving Girl Statue - © Brian Welker / 123rf.com

Forsyth Park Monument – © dndavis / deposit photos

Forsyth Park Fountain - © sepavone / deposit photos

First African Baptist - © kathyclark / deposit photos

Cathedral of St. John the Baptist - © James Pintar / 123rf.com

Congregation Mickve Israel - © dndavis / deposit photos

Bonaventure Cemetery – cross - © DeBuskPhoto / deposit photos

Bonaventure Cemetery – trees - © kreulen / deposit photos

Colonial Park Cemetery - © Hackman / deposit photos

Sea Turtle - © Patryk_Kosmider / deposit photos

Georgia State Railroad Museum - © Wilsilver77 / deposit photos

Old Fort Jackson – cannon - © Wilsilver77 / deposit photos

Fort Pulaski - © benkrut / deposit photos

Tybee Island Lighthouse Station - © duckeesue / deposit photos

ABOUT THE AUTHOR

Teresa Mills is the bestselling author of the "Hey Kids! Let's Visit..." Book Series for Kids!

Teresa's goal through her books and website is to help parents / grand-parents who want to build the life experiences of their children / grand-children through travel and learning activities.

She is an active mother and Mimi. She and her family love traveling in the USA, and internationally too! They love exploring new places, eating cool foods, and having yet another adventure as a family! With the Mills, it's all about traveling as family.

In addition to traveling, Teresa enjoys reading, hiking, biking, and helping others.

Join in the fun at
https://kid-friendly-family-vacations.com